from the kitchen floor

Emily Winters

from the kitchen floor

ISBN: 979-8-218-61908-4

Thanks, guys (you know who you are).

Guts

How you're made

We sit shoulder to shoulder and I
Pretend to love the silence and wonder if you'll notice.
I suppose a toleration of empty space and time is surely a
Deciding factor of who is "deep" and who is,
Unfortunately, "not:" lost causes, she says, leaves
Riding the stream taking her for all she's got and
Rationally, I know everyone has their shit and
Rationally, I know I don't know you or your shit.
First impressions are projections, leashes let loose a
Fraction of an inch at a time, slick leather
Bumping against blisters turned calluses and my
Skin, too, shrinks in
Poor weather -
Face taunt, reflection skeletal and my
Visage wavers so much, a tremble before a tumble, that
My stomach drops and I wonder if this glass is ancient or
If I'm just unknowable.
An ultimate dilemma if life is soap opera:
Moderately yet ambiguously successful young woman
Only discoverable in a series of common sense-defying
Mathematical gymnastics, stupefying equations.
A little girl only found in the fraction of a
Second before a raindrop
Hits hot pavement, the hiss felt more than heard.
It's only when I hold my ear closer to the grindstone to
Hear our moving parts - only as it sharpens me
Along with the knife do I twitch in the dark, a

Dog trapped in sleep, and what if they dream in code
Too? 0's and 1's, X's and O's?

He swipes fast before my eyes, groovy switching plates
Whetted fingers a blur, wet eyes more
Concept than emotion:
1 or 2? 2 or 1? Cat scratch quick.
A or B? B or A? And is it wrong to say
They all look the same to me?
And despite there being no correct answer to
This test, the optometrist levels such a look at me that
Lets me know I've failed all the same so I squint
Harder, try to
Pick out glints of sand or something that'll let me know
Which one's flawed or how they're made and you
Caught me staring.
Caught me trying to figure out how you're made and I
Still don't know how
Much you know or how she knows he knows
I know and the more
Childish the game, the more it stings because there's
Preciousness here or there could've been
Tenderness here.

Maybe we all judge too quickly as in
Sound wounds me but I've made a mortal enemy of
Silence after all the things it did to me: what
Populated my head, stared me in the
Face when you

Weren't around to collect my ugly things and
Fold them neatly at the foot of my bed or grip my
Elbow when I stumbled which softened my shoulders and
Loosened my knees and ultimately, added five more
Years onto my life, caboosed and tacked neatly onto the
End.
So, I thank you for that, but I sincerely
Wish that you'd leave me alone now because
I'm shredded into ribbons and I don't have the
Time, she says, or the "capacity" she says,
Brain on shutdown screen blacked-out expression in
Old glass redacted - to make me make
Sense to you because the you in my head that
Folds me origami and tucks me in your
Pocket and
Leaves my clothes neatly stacked at the foot of my bed
Already knows that I can't be tied into a bow and
I can't decorate fine spaces and I feel like a
Ghost in fine spaces, retreating conch-like
Into my bones, my soul becoming
Imperceptible, just
Traces of calcium, white and glossy in soft
Light, stretch marks tiger stripes
War wounds, and you trace me
Whelk-like I mean
Well, like I'm tracing paper and you hold me
Up to the light and ask yourself
1 or 2? Her or me or me or you? And that
Sounds like a *you* problem and it sounds like

An echoed shout a howl of joy or maybe,
Except in dreams, it sounds like nothing - but my dear
I'm just a leaf, after all, who
Didn't make the cut.
Limbless lifeless riding the stream, pretending
I love silence,
Pretending you love me.

Bell jar

Is my interest invasive?
Are my inquiries incessant obnoxious or
Endearing?
I only ever wanted a love, requited, but instead I
Find myself with spindly legs rather than
Dainty wings, stuttering rather than soaring.
The shape of my arms held above my head in
Silhouette is how I'd
Sketch your smirking mouth: a crooked charcoal
Slash in the
Darkness as it lowers itself over us.
I beat against this bell jar while you recline, happy to
Tarry inside your head.
I'm starting to think that the
Cages that capture captivate me can't
Hold you since you were never here in my bed or
At my kitchen table, instead burrowed away inside your
Mind just where your mother used to tuck you in
At night and you dug into
Another's worlds before
Growing more preoccupied with populating your
Own: when you've got a
Universe at your fingertips, what kind of
Everything could I offer you?

Sleep comes briefly, dispassionately, turbulently

To us both, but while you stay still to try to
Trick your body back into slumber, I fidget.
Beat drums into the sheets with numb feet, walk a
Mile, write and write, walk two miles, only to
Return and find you still motionless, flickering
Eyes under lids the shade of
Meat gone bad the only sign you'd
Ever been disturbed until one opens,
Pupil gaping maw wretched cave of
Dreams and destiny consuming your
Iris with the tenacity
Uncontrollability of a train blasting through a
Tunnel or a sinkhole devouring my
Crocs then my jeans then my sweatshirt then
Me—

When did I become so raw, bone on bone?
I seem to have gone bad too –
Morphed, Kafkaesque, molted and
Devolved under the bell jar next to you and
You watch with detached fascination as my
Final denouement takes shape and I wonder then if it
Was just my brain that had cast your interest as
Anything but profane. Instead of
Exalted, ecstatic, ecclesiastic, you just wanted to
See what would happen when you held a
Magnifying glass under the sun over me.

Imagine my surprise to find you just as

Intrigued by me as I am by you:
Except while I want to hold you, you want to
Hold me down.
One spindle leg of mine taps
Feebly at the glass,
Testing the water and we sleep fitfully,
Frustratingly foiled in both of our schemes and
Plans.

They say protagonists don't know the
Genre they inhabit, so I suppose this is what
Happens when my romantic comedy turns out to be a
Horror tragedy, and I suppose this is what
Happens when my
Sham coquettish surrender turns into a corpse
Stirred by the tide, melting on the
Shore -
Hair seaweed, my waterlogged features
Making me a prehistoric creature before I'm
Torn off, chewed, spit up - rotted repopulated then
I fly
Into the glass where I find myself watching you
Watching me fumble, stutter, and twitch,
Tables turned to such tragic results.

I'm not sure you took from me what I gave you.

Beatrice

Because I talk too much, I keep you in
My pocket, a precious gem to ponder in secret while the
Rest of my brain is paraded and exposed, tender
Tributaries parting under curious fingers like some
Sick party trick.

They won't be able to find you there.

I torture myself with the smallest moments, dwelling on a
Snapshot, still residing in the dwelling we once made our
Own under rock and stone.
Scrambling into the sun, I warm myself on the
Roof in the deep afternoon, glittering
Formica or fool's gold worming into my
Skin, pressing little divots into the
Backs of my thighs like fingerprints.

I wonder absently, pressing the bruise until it blooms
Black and blue behind my eyes too,
How long my body will have to remember you when my
Mind has long moved on?
Our bodies hold clues, your scars celestial multitudes or
Breadcrumbs to follow out of the woods, the way for me
To weigh what you've said and all that you never could:
Do you think Beatrice knew that she guided
Dante through Heaven?
Like houses with false fronts or folks waiting for the

Day to die, their grizzled hunched forms
Lurching on rocking chairs, running scarred
Tongues over false teeth, I built you, set your chair in
Motion with the lightest phantom touch -
Imbibed you, more concept than memory,
With my meaning.

My words in your mouth tumble through the
Gap in your teeth like loose gravel, too metaphorical of a
Diary to
Be of any true use, perhaps just
My way of creating problems to detangle,
Self-sabotage disguised as creativity,
Muses masked as lovers huddled deep inside my
Pocket.

Interlude

From the kitchen floor,
I watch you barefoot
Dancing again.

Our hands eek and creep towards each other
When we walk down the street and, I like to
Imagine,
In sleep: phototropic adjustments,
Evolutionary measures
Undertaken with intention.
We lean towards the sun before
Drunkenly tipping off our pedestals and
I catch you or
Maybe you caught me?
When I launched myself off a
Stoop, we cackled in the dark like
Only daylight lovers do.

Source-monitoring error

We want things even when they're no good for us,
She thinks, removing staples from
Briefs and memos before feeding them to the shredder.
They fold easily, bending at the whim of metal jaws.
Would it really be all that better if someone covered me
With their body, held mse down
Bug under a cup or scooped me up on their
Way downtown?

Residing resentfully inside her cocoon, she
Listens to the chatter drifting over the top of the
Cubicle, the faces of her nieces and nephews
Mocking her from the back of a best friend's family's
Boat, push pin puncturing where the sun would've
Been.
I'd be good. I promise.
Punctuating what was probably an inane point or
Something casually cruel with empty air, the
Conversation comes to an
Abrupt end after her colleagues feel
Her curious gaze, extending over the vinyl wall,
Snail eyes: attentive and curious, pupils tracking
Stocks or counting the dinners she'd never been
Invited to with generally genial moseying.

As staple after staple is plucked with dexterity,
She foments aggressive daydreams, picking and

16

Gnawing at memories of silences and stares or the
Time she ate her way through
Two Lean Cuisine meals at a time.
Fermenting in the corner of the office behind the
Water cooler, her molecules buzz like the cheap
Fluorescent lighting and if she were
Protozoa, she probably wouldn't have been
Capable of surviving the heat as her cells shook.
She imagined her tiny self,
Nucleus and all,
Bursting into flames behind the dehydrated
Spider plant and shuddered.

Maybe it would be good for me.

Like her microscopic brethren,
She filter feeds, sorting through information,
Unconsciously spinning fairytales and regurgitating them
For whoever cares enough to listen and after a
While, all the words look similar and if
Asked under oath, she would
Have sworn it was something Ben next door had
Whispered, not something she'd read once in a used
Paperback thriller.

Maybe you'd be good for me.

She too was a source-monitoring error: misinterpreted,
Misremembered, misattributed - easily forgotten then

Rewritten depending on the ending of the story,
Whatever it takes for the folks standing
Stiffly in a polite row at the back of the room to
Feel righteous as they pay their respects.

She supposed she was a lyric from a song
Overplayed to exhaustion, taken for granted until you
Couldn't even hear her anymore, so
Why not indulge a
Main character moment? In a year or two they
Wouldn't really be her words or her memories anymore
Anyway,
Just rumors whispered over cubicles or by
Bathroom doors.

Sea swallow

The sea slug *Glaucus atlanticus*
Offhandedly referred to as
Blue angel
Blue dragon or
Sea swallow can
Topple a Man of War several times the
Size of its body and take its venom to
Wield against their own predators.

Is it possible for me, too, to eat my fear and
Become it?

In the daylight, I shrivel up and die a little
When you touch me, sensory overload in
Summer heat.
You're the salt in my wound the salt of the
Earth, the taste that pools above my top lip.
The sea air on bare skin
Turns me crustacean, grows on me like
Rock candy, and I lay on the sand and pray I
Become a monument sooner rather than
Later, a snack for you in the afternoon or
Better still, an artifact for some kids to find when they
Trip over my half hidden knees or a
Single finger poised in accusation or observation
Rising Lady Liberty from the sand.
In my finest hour, deep in that suspended

Not quite posthumous bliss, science would
Take my body if you didn't beat them to it:
Cheery cherry red shovels eviscerate my
Skin, the plastic bending before breaking
Through my shell, an autopsy in primary
Colors and curious coconut-scented fingers.

I've put up such a front that my pick up lines
Sound closer to sandpipers rustling amongst
Dunes than skin on skin, and sure, I can protect my
Lungs from eroding but soon I'll bury you too,
Close you off inside of me with
Some vague consideration that if I eat the thing that
Hurts me, I can overcome it:
Neutralize the threat
Acid turned basic
Sunshine turned amiable or rather,
Tolerable, and I'll try not to
Think of the time back when the door to the
Balcony locked from the outside and I
Fried on the concrete waiting to be remembered, an
Old dog in the heat
Windows up
Mercy killing you know and the sun too turned
Me crustacean and your fingers
Wiggled in the cracks and broke me
Open. You devoured bits of me when it
Pleased you, hoarding the best for last, for an
Ending that would never be realized -

If I could stand the burn of swallowing the sun or
Chomping you whole as you slept unsteady, the
Rise and fall of your chest a choppy
Sea, then would I be able to burn you out of me?
But what if I eat the thing I hate and become it?

Do I like myself when no one is around to
tell me I should?

Tender

I know to take the things you say when you are
Scared with a healthy dose of skepticism.
You aren't in your right mind, your body dwarfed by the
Hulking complications of your life.
But the scrutiny wears my limbs
Until you can see straight through threads of
Muscle and bone without achieving any more
Clarity than before, and my mind is a freight train.
No matter how close I
Crush my body to the wall, it still draws blood as it
Oozes past, both incredibly slow and immediate, a
Black and
Blue blur and I see what you're going to say reflected in
Your eyes before you say it, excuses and
Self-deprecations and lies you wouldn't really call
Lies peppering me in slow motion, and on our
Worst days, I wish I could offer my body to
Science, wondering in that
Sick way of someone who's never taken a punch that if I
Taunt and bite and kick and if I screech
Fight me, hit me, if you would, and if
It would make you feel better to lash out with
More concrete consequences, so you can see the
Blood, rather than so easily forget the
Blooming bruises, my tender skin after your
Words burrow and tuck themselves in next to the
Razor blades next to the diamonds sharp and

23

Prickly, and they
Fortify their defenses so that I flinch before you
Speak, and I anticipate all the ways you'll say *it's
Not you, it's me*, and now you can't
Touch me without it hurting,
Because I already miss you, and I've already
Mourned you, and
I already feel your side of the bed warm yet empty, the
Breeze from the window crisping your pillow faster than I
Can clutch it to my chest and try to steal some of your
Lingering breaths.
So, I know how to live through your fears, and I
Know how to say *I understand*.
But as the offenses mount and the
Sediment at the bottom compounds without
Stirring, I'm not sure I know how to survive and
I'm not sure I know how to be the only one of us
Left alive.

Interluditude

The sounds of cicadas
Begrudgingly emerging from the
Underground mimic the sounds that fall out of
Your mouth, your bottom lip a
Slotted spoon, your saliva soup.

Our shapes are silly in
Silhouette as I headbutt your arm in fondness,
Not a territorial statement or a
Declaration of war. Not this time.

Another poem about just some boy

You know the one, the one that
Makes you rearrange your words before they mushroom
Ooze from your tongue, mad libs mad cap
Chopped and diced in the pocket-sized food er word er
Food processor I
Tuck in my sheets with me before
Reanimating my best shiny stitched-up
Monstrous similes and sending them for a stuttering walk
Down the block and in through your window.
My phone is
Suspended dangerously from my aching fingers or
Resting on my chest steaming and
Irradiating my breasts, probably, and I'm abducted by the
Frost-bit white blur,
Imagining you contemplating my words, thinking of an
Artfully louche reply to make me think
You don't care too much or
Maybe I'm too much of a
Sucker to realize that you really don't care that much
Huh
You know the one - the one that makes you
Contemplate your wardrobe, the way you
Take up space how casual looks on you but
If asked he'd say he
Never asked, he just said he likes girls who
Aren't afraid to eat, likes girls who
Don't wear makeup likes girls who

Don't dress like sluts but girls who
Actually care and tweeze and girls who think about
How they take up space but no, he
Never asked you to change for spare change for a
Meal on the table every night and I'd come
Bounding anyway, meet you at the
Door the most well-trained pooch cooch cunt
You've ever seen, I mean since you never asked, really.

Do all fungi have gills and do they have
Gills because they
Breathe underwater or breed under the water and
If we have sex in your bathtub does that mean I need
Them too? What about that time you held me under
Faucet under
Lily-pad facsimile etched from soap scum and I became
Microscopic, bug-eyed and the parasites
From your bachelor pond found my pores and
Bounced trampoline off my ear drums until I heard
Nothing, felt your
Noxious expirations through your hands on my neck and
Realized that
You couldn't breathe for me after all.

I wonder if the other
Micromycetes feel safety in numbers or are
Devastated by the masses that
All experience the same, shot out spit spritz and
I wonder if the

Myrmidons felt betrayed to go to war for the glory of
their
Leader for a
Woman they'd never know or if they felt the same
Desire and ownership for her concept as
Menelaus. Did they hunger for that something more -
that
Boot on back those hands-on neck - the
I never asked but she just did?
Were they consumed by the King of Mycenae's
Ugly virulence and violence? The sort long since
Dog-earred, noted then
Forgotten, excused by popular memory, my
Denigration through your
Absence echoing in print, speckled through the
Frost-bit white blur and it was
Just an accident, a
Directionless blameless tragedy as if my
Spores were grown in a lab void of social control.
All because he was
Just some boy, he escaped nameless, while
I am shunned, shamed, and
Trampled and still they fuck me because even if he didn't
Ask for it she sure
Did.

Nymph

Spectator today, the armrests tease into my thighs before
Giving a sigh of relief imperceptible to my
Neighbors as my body
Slips between vinyl borders,
Settling into a seat the color and texture of
Curdled merlot.
Grotesque movements flip their way in through
My irises before righting themselves on the
Backside of my brain, projector screen stretched taut,
Resting against meninges the texture of asbestos.
The images never seem to penetrate to the
Arachnoid despite the way the dancers
Skitter along invisible webs, their
Twitching bodies mimicking
Fingers picking their way through a Chopin waltz.

Contorted in fractured lighting, their naked ankles are
Precisely quirked and in the
Glare from the stage lights, I see things with
Hard shells squirming, ready to
Pop from chromatic calves, flexing, relaxing -
Tensed to spring from the chrysalis of a
Dancer's skin.
Veins protrude from necks like lines of
Aggressive emphasis from an
Overenthusiastic editor and as a child, I wonder if

I would have accepted such feedback with open
Ears.
Watching the show, I wonder whether I ever
Noted the sly body modifications, the way I
Crafted and created and grew into a
Body that wasn't really my own, even as I
Scorned and scoffed and
Silently judged when my cohort
Changed themselves for others.

My arm rubs against someone that I used to know or
At least they
Used to know me and
I think then about how brothers or
Mothers may always see you half the child half
Still dependent yet too old to be so.
The couples on the stage promenade,
Gears artfully hidden, calluses creaking and cracking and
Hardening more against the solid gray floor.
The dancers huddle and creep across the stage.
The thirteen right arms of this strange commune
Crookedly lift like an
Insect's legs and I wonder
Whose crucible this was, their
Make or break moment as they
Mimed gossiping mandibles.
I wonder if they feel the
Things waiting to sprout from their bodies,
Self-deprecations that adapt as we age like

Bunions or maybe more of that self-imposed
Loneliness, the feral desperation for *more*.

I shiver in the anticipation and glee that winds up and
Around the auditorium, electrifying or paralyzing
Us all like tape or
Leotard, stockings, hair net, hairspray -
All the things that kept down the
Parts of us that would
Jiggle or giggle.
We watch breathless,
Gleefully horrified as the
Nymphs crack and break into dragonflies cast in
Pearlescent blues and greens.
My nose and fingers are cold, my bones aching as
I clutch onto the armrests and
Watch, transfixed, wondering
Whether I could have ever been that good.

Tender: Deux

I know to take the things I think when I am
Scared with a healthy dose of skepticism.
I'm not in the right mind, the right form:
Disembodied, a faint shout from a
Distant room and if you'd
Follow, I'd like to be the
Shiver that
Crosses your skin when you
Walk through the door.
Imagine if I made believers of us both?
My hands are arthritic actors, shades and shadows of the
Tools they were before, and I cast my
Hauntings along hallways and across wallpaper, roaming
In the night,
Ruminating in the night
Eating our dreams
Nosferatu lurching creaking crawling creeping and I've
Tried my best not to be just another stain
Left on the tracks after a freight train draws blood as
It slaps past,
Tried my best not to become my
Passing thoughts but I've become a burr in your
Side after all, haven't I?
But these are yet more fantastical fabrications,
Self-deprecations and lies I wouldn't really call
Lies a heavy blanket pulled up to your chin and you

Peak above the cotton and I peer back from the
Corner, caged and cagey and feral, unfit for
Human perception. Even yours. Especially yours.
On my worst days, I wish I could offer my body to science,
Wondering in that sick way of someone who's lost
Feeling in their limbs from too many minutes and hours
Astray whether
Being poked and prodded would bring me
Back to my senses or at the very least,
Whether I could be a cure for something and
Be of some use, finally.
I wonder if it would make me feel better to
Lash out with more
Concrete consequences, so I could see the blood,
Watch as my words burrow next to your defenses,
Festering next to stakes and silver bullets and
Chevaux de frise.
Somehow I snuck underneath the
Covers with you, never tripped the bells hung with
Obsessive perfection around the room.
But now the window is open and its nearing dawn and
I wonder:
Have you already mourned me? My side of the bed still
Warm yet empty.
A lonely breeze crisps my pillow
Faster than you could savor any lingering breaths and,
You see,
I know how to breathe through my fears, and
I know I shouldn't

Believe the things I think when they rattle their chains,
Shake their fists but I'm not sure I know how to
Hide you from my worst self:
I'm not sure I know how to be the only one of us living
Dead.

I think I made myself smaller than you ever did.

Growing pains

Are independence and self-reliance something that
Grows? What to do when our earth is
Fallow, our bodies barren and why is it so easy to
Call myself a lost cause when I know others are
Gardens of unlimited potential?

We've hit rocky ground cement foundation and
No amount of digging will do.

What I mean to say is:
I should be honest about what I think and
Feel and what I hate and what drives me
Insane, put words to the ensnaring
Metaverse inside my head –

No. What I mean to say is:
I have nothing left to give.

Ripped off hunks of myself, dropped them at your
Feet, walked away with the idea of
My hands raised in surrender – not take me as I
Am but take whatever part you'd like and
Discard the rest,
Leave it for the scavengers or carrier pigeons,
Bread collecting must and mildew in the
Gutter and I'd say get your mind out of it but
I give other people my body too, free access

Unlimited no warranty endless swipes so that they
Don't feel rejected or feel less than human and
I'm only what you make me:
Boogeyman or
A dream and I play make believe too.
Fiercely, clinging to fading
Tendrils of sleep, I wish into reality the
Things you whispered to me after hours.

But the thoughts above this last line are just
Aggressive fabrications.
Postpartum disappointments when people don't
Behave the way they did in my head.

You are not only what I make of you.

I'm estranged to myself, though folks usually just call this
"Growing pains."
But I remember aching ankles and knees, chest but
I don't remember ever burrowing quite so deep before,
Don't remember being such a push over the edge of the
Platform before:
Sparing people vitriol or, more mildly, foregoing honesty,
Giving the blunt edge of my sword because
I think a bruise on my own palm
Bubbling and popping with callouses is
Better than you bleeding out on the floor, the
Flick of my wrist
Orchestrated intentional nothing ever casual as I

Sacrifice the moment of truth to save the story.
Not to mention, I suppose that cutting you would just
Piss me off, in the end, if you got your wine on my
Bread on the linoleum disguised as hardwood though
Perhaps it would thrill and intrigue me if we
Made holy communion on the kitchen floor but
I'm not sure if you'd prefer to dine and dash, to swipe
Left and how could you say no one ever chooses you?
The voices ask me, vague and insubstantial,
Moving in and out of my life with the entitlement only
Strangers can possess like Charlie Brown adults and
All I hear is
Wa wah wah wah and they choose
Ideas of me, and they choose me but they choose
More them than me anyway.

And I've been too eager to fit myself into
Other people's lives, flattered I'd aced the
Line up, well on my way to perfecting and
Mastering friendship, pleased that they'd
Passed my trip wires and
Vetting, the myriad of ways I
Put you to the test though you'd never guess.
I never thought being a
"Pick me girl" with friends is being a pick me
Girl but here we are and I'm alone,
Racing ruminations in the pouring rain like a sad,
Tried and true and treasured cliché, and it feels like six
More weeks of winter here

Feels like the feels like.
Basket crumbly bits of loose chips rattling around
Popped bag, what's left of my
Excitement and anticipation and stupidly, I put my
Eggs into your basket and I guess this is
What happens when we get big and old and yet,
Despite all this,
I still sit at home and wonder if you could
Make my garden grow.

Sweetness too

I want to eat the little moments with you and then
My insides will never be cold.
I want to cohabitate
Narrow ledges and wide vistas,
Galley kitchens and crowded
Closet bathrooms. I want to
Isolate the devastation in your brain and
Build it a little room that you can visit when and
If you are ready.
I want to insulate you from the chill,
Block wind and sun, my body a blanket or an
Old yellow beach towel crumbled up and tossed
On the back seat.

Shade and shadow can be sweetness too: pockets of
Darkness hidden about the bed, flirting with
Sun spots on white cotton;
Cool damp cradles beneath rocks where lively things
Grow;
Pebbles in knees as I bend to inspect
Something squishy and wet,
Pebbles on skin from cavern air or the
Hair on your arm brushing my own (maybe we've been
Grown here too).

I'm fond of you so maybe I should let things go
Like a slotted spoon too, clutch onto you in

Gentle compassion and awareness of the universes
That thrive behind your melting eyes, not capture or
Memorialize or mount you pinned wings onto the wall.

I will leave the selfish desperation that threatened to
Stain my love standing still and suspicious by the
Roadside,
Sentinel, parasite, hitchhiker to go
Pollute the next fool who
Fumbles in fear down those same streets.
I'll toss the intrusive thoughts
Off my shoulders out the window as we
Fly down the interstate like a bandana snatched from
My hand, flag of truce, a promise to stop, to listen, to
Warm your hands under my thighs if you asked.

I embrace you from behind to
Feel your lungs expand through my chest so that I can
Know that you are breathing, know that I am
Breathing and you
Catch my stare and I bloom, mushrooms in caves a
Thousand shades and in silent looks, I ask you to
Forage me,
Forgive me, or let me know where to come
Collect you at the
End of the night when the roads are deserted and the
Air is buzzing with whispers of stories yet unfinished.

Art museum

And I think at the start a part of me thought
You would swoop in and fix me,
Deus ex machina.
But that's not really fair, is it - can there be
Love without Ego, without subterfuge
Acting, without feeling like we wear out our
Welcome when we say what's on our minds or
Feel like a fraud when we tell silly little lies?
Though they quickly build, weaving around themselves,
Becoming fraying tapestries heavy and ripe with
Time.
They are suspended above our heads on
Hidden metal hooks and I wait for
These rugs to plummet and crush us with history.

You sit still and gaze in reverence at
Beautiful things
Made by wizened wise fingers while I sit still and
Gaze at you. Your eyes
Glisten as if an ancient seamstress had pressed her
Knowledge onto your waiting tongue
Communion wafer carried aloft with
Skilled yet aching fingers and she touches you with the
Rich respect that comes with sensing that we are
Unknowable to one another and accepting it.

I long to accept it: to take you as you are and take

Me as I am - to shut it down, isolate and
Heal the
Spindly things that have always matched my vertebrae
Step for step,
Unfurling and stabbing me with every breath.
These insecure bony things, these
Maladaptations chased the
Pieces of you around my heart and
Tried to ensnare us both, strap us to
Ventricles and we
Would've died there without the
Sunlight bouncing off these
White walls and I am a present thing,
Walking these halls with you and
Pretending to be able to read when I can't
Even see, blinded by the way I can't stop
Thinking about you, the human, as you
Touch the small of my back, leaning close to
Whisper something insightful or maybe
Insulting about the
Art before us and it's then that my
Head catches up to the plot: you and I are not a
Work of art.

Rather than push more words into our
Atmosphere, I laugh instead and pull you closer.

About the author

Emily Winters (she/her) works at a historic site in Philadelphia by day and is a rambling poet and painter by night. She was raised in a small (no stoplight) town in South Jersey. She enjoys late-night dessert runs with friends and long hikes in the woods. Though previously published in New Jersey Bards Poetry Review and Spark to Flame, a Journal of Collaborative Poetry, this is her first published poetry collection.

Emily can be reached at em.winters.writes@gmail.com.